To: _____

From: _____

For those who feel the sun rises and sets on their grandchildren.

Blue Balloon
BOOKS

My Grandson

Copyright © 2025 by Jackie Winkelmann
Illustrations by artist Eszter Szepvolgyi, represented by Beehive Illustration

ISBN 979-8-9861919-3-5 (Hardcover)
ISBN 979-8-9861919-2-8 (Paperback)

Printed in the United States of America

This book was produced and published in partnership with
Blue Balloon Books, an imprint of Ballast Books.

www.blueballoonbooks.com

For my best boys, Wade, Tyler, and Cooper,
who open my eyes to the magic in everyday life.

My grandson is the
best grandson.

He brightens the room and warms my heart.
He gives each day a shining start.

I like to take him wherever I go.

We laugh and play as
I watch him grow.

He is helpful.
He is kind.

He is the most amazing grandson you will ever find.

He is smart and silly
and so much fun.

Yes, my **grandson**
is number one!

He is friendly
and full of joy.

Oh, my grandson is the greatest boy!

Even when things
don't go his way . . .

. . . he knows tomorrow
will be a new day.

Sometimes, we cook or
bake a sweet treat,

a treat my grandson
likes to eat.

We dance and sing
until the day is done.

My grandson is
the finest one!

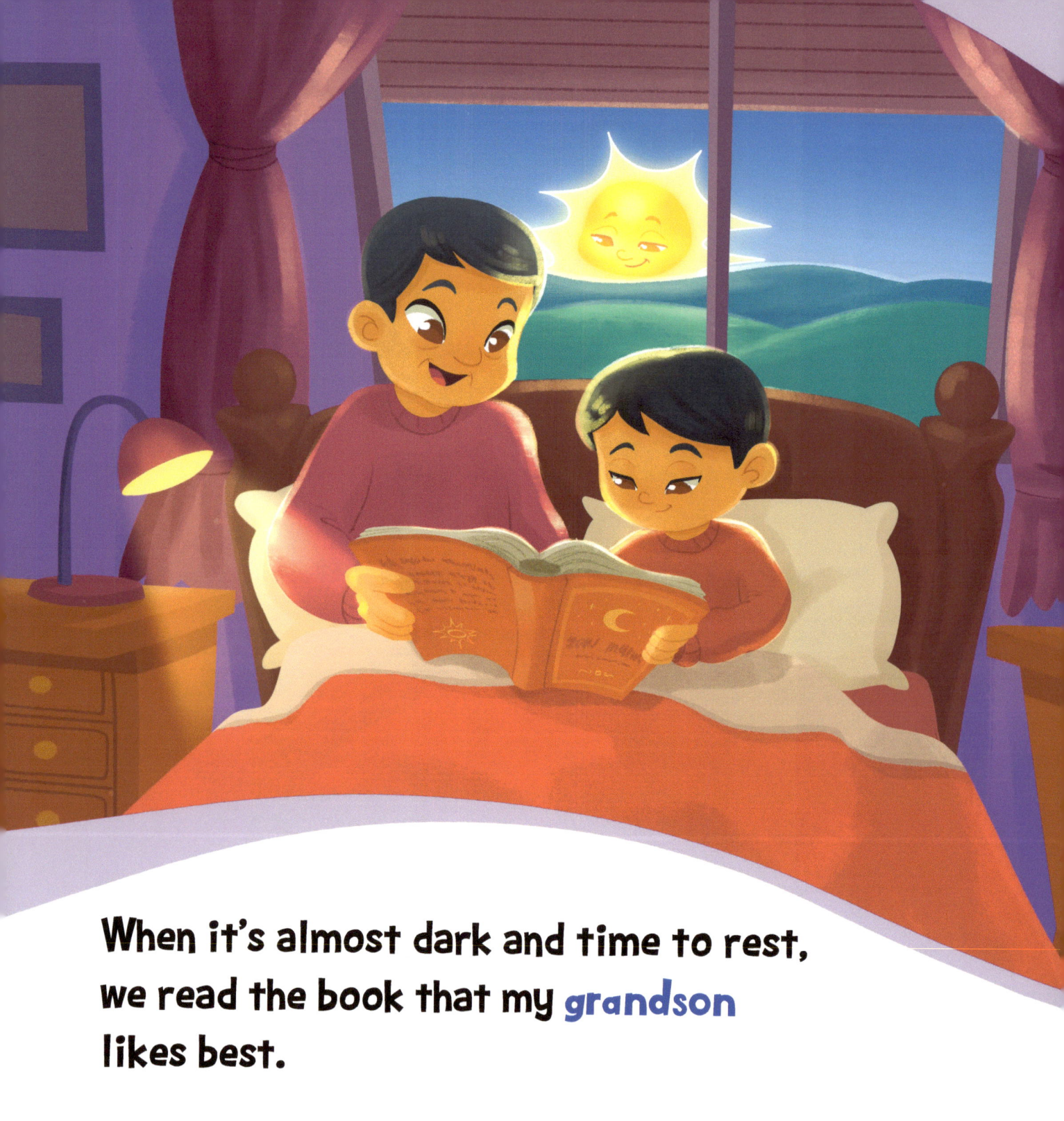

When it's almost dark and time to rest, we read the book that my grandson likes best.

Then, we hug real tight and say good night,
looking forward to the morning light.

My **grandson** is grand indeed, the grandest **grandson** there ever will be.

How do I know
this is true?

Because . . .
my grandson is YOU!

Search and Find

 pie  camera  cowboy hat  tennis racket  sword

 soccer ball  octopus  sunflower  kite rocket

Jackie Winkelmann has privately shared her creativity with family and friends for many years. She loves to transform everyday life events into warm stories, funny rhymes, and heartfelt greeting cards. Jackie is a registered nurse who lives with her husband in Texas. She is the proud mother of two amazing daughters and now has five wonderful grandchildren, who are the inspiration for many of her stories. She is now thrilled to publish her children's book *My Grandson*. In addition to writing, Jackie enjoys spending time with family and friends, being outdoors, and traveling.